ELECTRIFIED!

CONDUCTORS AND INSULATORS

Gareth Stevens
Publishing

By C. O. Shea

Please visit our website, www.garethstevens.com. For a free color catalog of all our high-quality books, call toll free 1-800-542-2595 or fax 1-877-542-2596.

Library of Congress Cataloging-in-Publication Data

Shea, C. O., 1978-
  Conductors and insulators / C.O. Shea.
      pages cm. — (Electrified!)
  Includes bibliographical references and index.
  ISBN 978-1-4339-8390-0 (paperback)
  ISBN 978-1-4339-8391-7 (6-pack)
  ISBN 978-1-4339-8389-4 (library binding)
  1. Electric conductors—Juvenile literature. 2. Electric currents—Juvenile literature. 3. Semiconductors—Juvenile literature. I. Title.
  TK3303.S54 2013
  621.3—dc23
                                        2012019597

First Edition

Published in 2013 by
Gareth Stevens Publishing
111 East 14th Street, Suite 349
New York, NY 10003

Copyright © 2013 Gareth Stevens Publishing

Designer: Katelyn E. Reynolds
Editor: Therese Shea

Photo credits: Cover, p. 1 Triff/Shutterstock.com; cover, pp. 1 (logo), 5, 11, 21 iStockphoto/Thinkstock.com; cover, pp. 1, 3–24 (background) Lukas Radavicius/Shutterstock.com; cover, pp. 1, 3–24 (image frame) VikaSuh/Shutterstock.com; p. 7 Encyclopaedia Britannica/UIG/Getty Images; p. 9 Comstock/Thinkstock.com; p. 13 Jim Barber/Shutterstock.com; p. 15 neijia/Shutterstock.com; p. 17 Bobkeenan Photography/Shutterstock.com; p. 19 Graham Reading/Photoshot/Getty Images.

Printed in the United States of America

CPSIA compliance information: Batch #CW13GS: For further information contact Gareth Stevens, New York, New York at 1-800-542-2595.

CONTENTS

Words in the glossary appear in **bold** type the first time they are used in the text.

ENERGY ALL AROUND

When you think of electricity, you probably think of the power that makes your TV or computer work. Electricity powers many of our **devices**, but it's a part of nature, too. Electrical force is found in every bit of matter in the universe! In fact, it holds together the **particles** that make up matter.

In the 1800s, people found out how to use electrical power, or energy, to make light, heat, and motion. Ever since, electricity has made our lives easier—and more fun!

POWER FACT!

Electricity is even found in the human body. It tells our heart to beat!

BUILDING MATTER

Matter is made up of atoms. Atoms are too small to be seen with the human eye. An atom is so tiny that a million atoms side by side are about as wide as a human hair! Atoms are made up of even tinier particles called electrons, neutrons, and protons. Protons and neutrons make up the **core**, or nucleus, of the atom. Electrons circle the nucleus.

Usually, an atom has the same number of protons and electrons. However, an atom can gain or lose electrons.

POWER FACT!

Neutrons and protons are made up of even smaller particles called quarks.

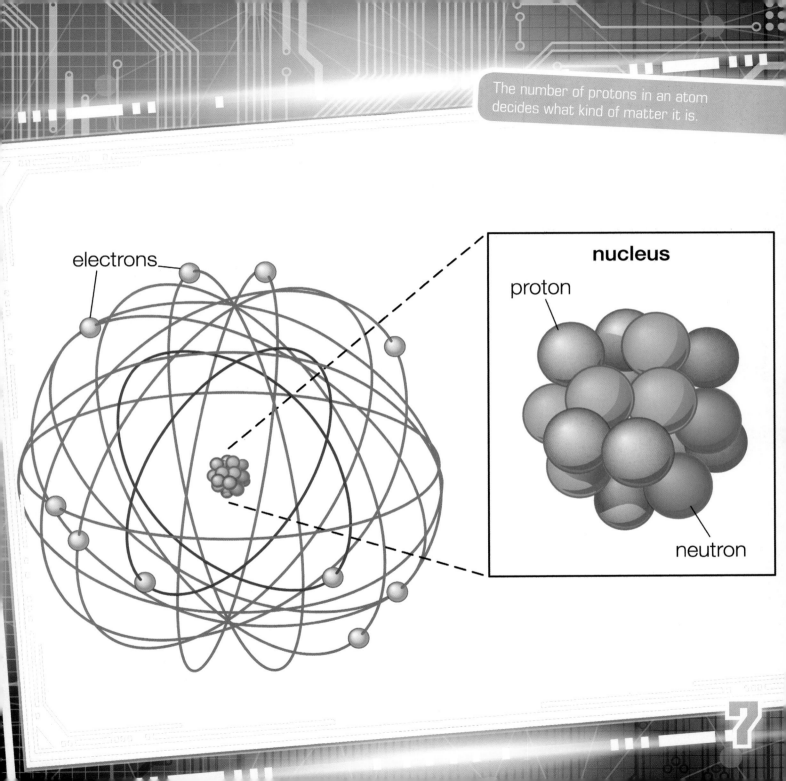

electrons

nucleus

proton

neutron

WHAT IS A CURRENT?

A flow of free electrons is called an electric current. The moving electrons carry energy from one point to another. When we need electricity to power our devices, we use a **charge** to begin the flow of a current. The charge causes electrons to pop off their atoms and flow through matter, powering our devices.

However, a current won't flow through all matter. Materials can be grouped according to their ability to carry an electric current.

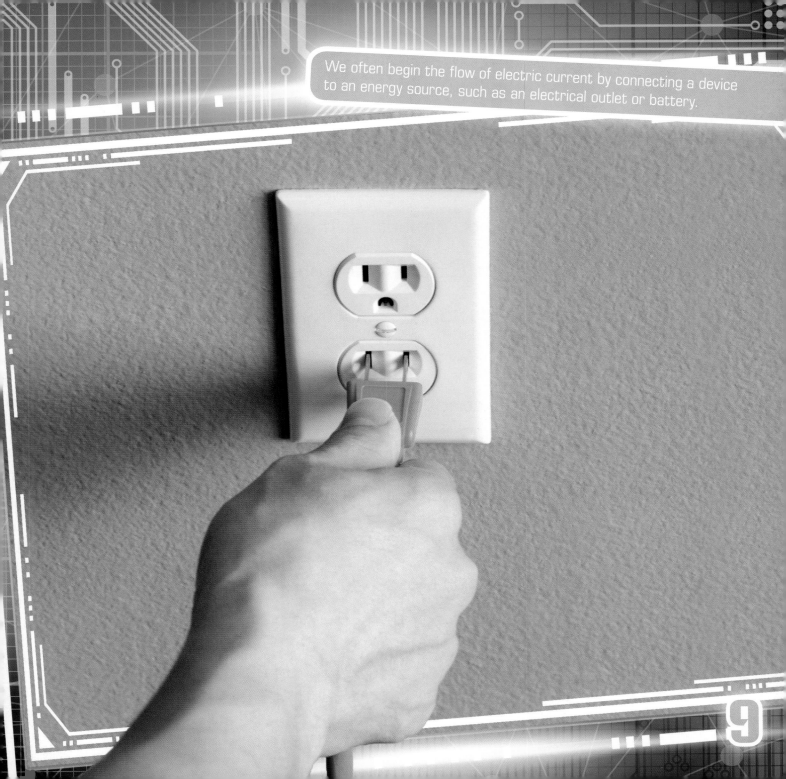

We often begin the flow of electric current by connecting a device to an energy source, such as an electrical outlet or battery.

CONDUCTORS

Materials that easily allow an electric current to flow through them are called conductors. The conductor carries, or conducts, an electric current. When an electric charge is introduced to the conductor, free electrons travel through the material.

Metals are good conductors. Electrons in metals leave their atoms and move through the matter easily. This is why most electrical wires are made of metal, such as copper. Lead and tin are metals, but they're poor conductors. They don't lose their electrons as easily.

POWER FACT!

An atom that has more or fewer electrons than normal is called an ion.

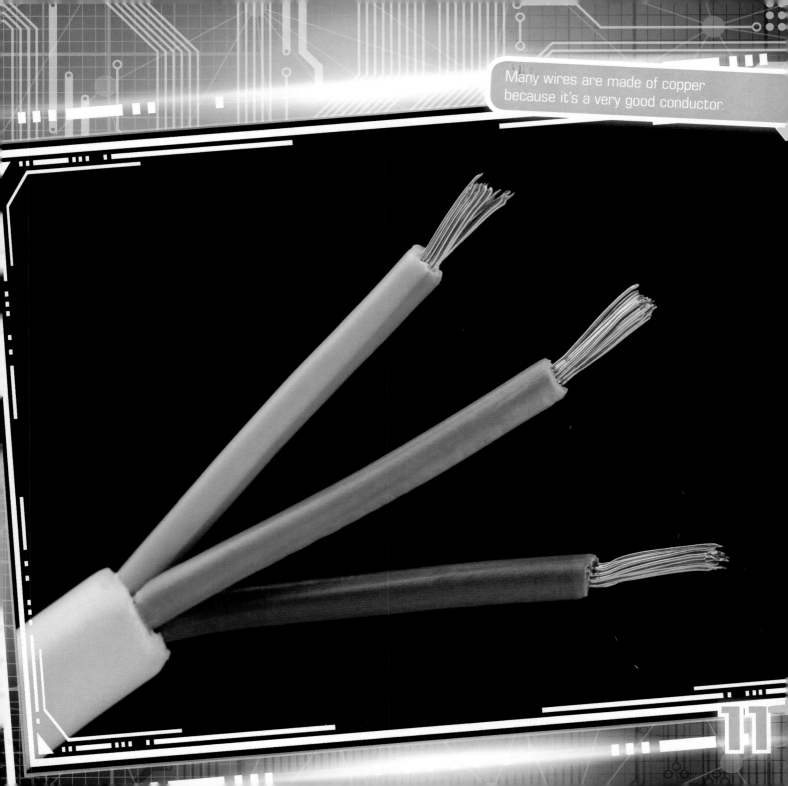

Many wires are made of copper because it's a very good conductor.

INSULATORS

In materials called insulators, electrons stick tightly to their atoms and don't travel around. When an electric charge is applied to an insulator, nothing happens. There is no electric current. Insulators include glass, rubber, plastic, and dry wood.

Have you ever noticed the material on the outside of an electrical cord? It's usually plastic or rubber so that you won't get shocked if you touch it. The current runs through the conductor inside the cord, while the insulator keeps the electricity from traveling outside.

COMMON CONDUCTORS AND INSULATORS

CONDUCTORS	INSULATORS
copper	dry wood
water	glass
silver	rubber
aluminum	plastic

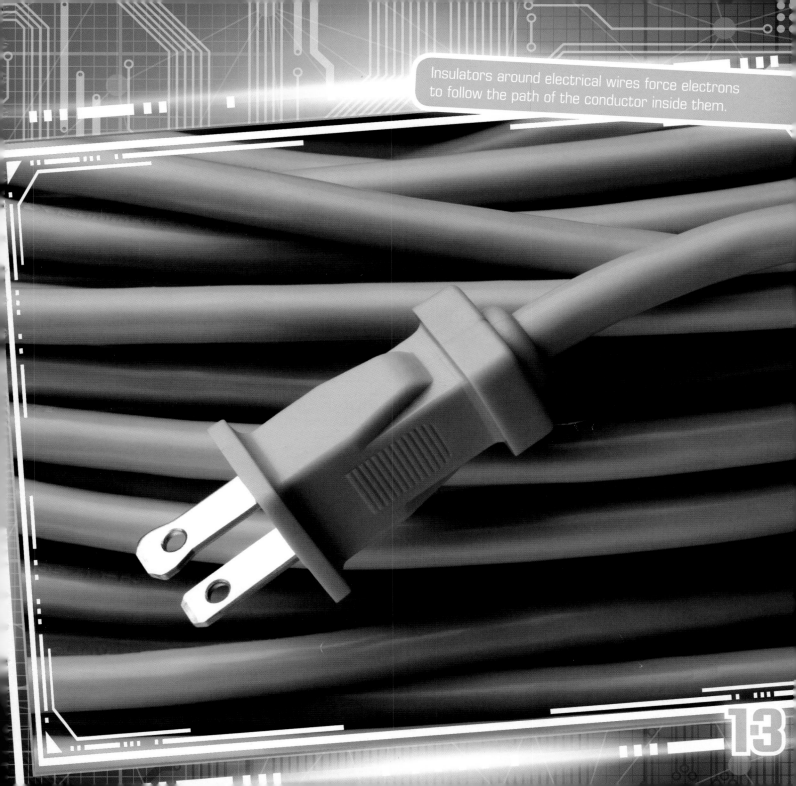

Insulators around electrical wires force electrons to follow the path of the conductor inside them.

13

SEMICONDUCTORS

Some materials fall somewhere between the groupings of conductors and insulators. These are called semiconductors. Matter can be added to semiconductors to increase their ability to conduct electricity.

Silicon is a semiconductor. It's an element that wouldn't normally lose its electrons. However, when certain matter is added to silicon, its nature changes. It allows a flow of current that can be controlled more easily than through metal conductors. Semiconductors such as silicon are used in computers, TVs, and gaming systems.

Silicon is also used to make solar cells, which are
devices that change the sun's energy to electricity.

15

PLASMAS

If a gas is hot enough, its atoms move very, very fast. As they hit each other, their electrons break free. When this happens, the gas becomes a **plasma**. Plasma is a conductor. It's seen in just a few places in nature, such as lightning, the sun, and stars.

An electric current can also make a plasma. You've probably seen neon signs in store windows. An electric charge flows through the gas in the sign and turns it into a plasma. The plasma's electric energy becomes light energy.

POWER FACT!

Plasma isn't considered a solid, liquid, or gas.

SUPERCONDUCTORS

When electrons flow through conductors, plasmas, and semiconductors, they lose energy. A superconductor is a material electrons can move through without losing energy. They only work in extreme **temperatures**, so they aren't used often. They power certain trains and medical devices, however.

Scientists are working on ways to bring superconductors into everyday use. Many people think superconductors could solve today's pollution problems and cut down on power shortages.

POWER FACT!

In 2000, scientists Andre Geim and Sir Michael Berry used a superconductor to **levitate** a frog!

Maglev trains use superconductors and magnets to raise train cars above the tracks.

YOU'RE A CONDUCTOR!

Water is a conductor, which is why you need to get out of the pool during a lightning storm. Water could conduct electricity right through you! You could be greatly harmed or even killed.

Since the human body contains about 60 percent water, you're a conductor, too! That's why you should *never* touch a wire that may be live. Electricity naturally flows to the ground. The current may travel through your body to reach the ground. Always be very careful around electricity.

Electrical workers wear special gloves and suits to keep them safe while they work near power lines.

21

GLOSSARY

charge: an amount of electricity

core: the central part of something

device: a tool or machine made to perform a task

levitate: to cause to rise and float in the air

particle: a very small piece of something

plasma: a hot gas made up of ions and electrons

temperature: how hot or cold something is

FOR MORE INFORMATION

Books

McGregor, Harriet. *Electricity.* New York, NY: Windmill Books, 2011.

Pegis, Jessica. *What Are Insulators and Conductors?* New York, NY: Crabtree Publishing, 2012.

Riley, Peter D. *Circuits & Conductors.* North Mankato, MN: Smart Apple Media, 2008.

Websites

Conductors and Insulators
www.fplsafetyworld.com/?ver=kkblue&utilid=fplforkids&id=16185
Read a long list of conductors and insulators, and learn more about electricity.

Electricity: Conductors and Insulators
www.quia.com/cm/25645.html
Play a game to test your knowledge of conductors and insulators.

INDEX